COOL MIND

COOL

 Shambhala   Boulder   2016

MIND

11 Easy Ways to Relieve Stress, Boost Self-Confidence, and Improve Concentration in School, Sports, and Life

DAVID KEEFE

Shambhala Publications, Inc.
4720 Walnut Street
Boulder, Colorado 80301
www.shambhala.com

9 8 7 6 5 4 3 2 1

First US Edition
Printed in the United States of America

♾ This edition is printed on acid-free paper that meets the
American National Standards Institute Z39.48 Standard.
♻ Shambhala makes every effort to print on recycled paper.
For more information please visit www.shambhala.com.

Distributed in the United States by Penguin Random House LLC
and in Canada by Random House of Canada Ltd

Designed by Jonathan Sainsbury // 6x9design

Library of Congress Cataloging-in-Publication Data

Keefe, David, 1966–
Cool mind: 11 easy ways to relieve stress, boost self-confidence, and
improve concentration in school, sports, and life / David Keefe.—
First American edition.
pages   cm
Originally published in 2011 by Exisle Publishing, Wollombi, Australia.
ISBN 978-1-61180-301-3 (paperback)
1. Stress management. 2. Relaxation. 3. Meditation. I. Title.
RA785.K436 2016
158.1'28—dc23
2015021861

CONTENTS

Your teacher is putting the exam papers in front of you, and you're starting to stress. You have only a few minutes to get yourself together before the exam begins. How do you stay calm?

At a party, someone you like is walking your way. You always seem to get nervous about dating, so how do you stay cool and not make a fool out of yourself?

Your competitors in the basketball final look pretty determined. They're staring you down. How do you stay focused and rise above it all?

Are you fed up with being nervous and full of self-doubt? Do you wonder how you will ever feel confident and comfortable with yourself?

Are you bursting with energy to try something new but feeling the same old nerves and doubts making you freeze up?

If any of these situations seem familiar, then you have found the right little book, because this book is all about the art of relaxing, the art of consciously becoming calm and cool *now,* to rise above stress. And the good news is it's not difficult! Read on and find out.

COOL MIND

WHAT IS A COOL MIND?

This book is a crash course in becoming cool and calm no matter what's going on in your life. It only takes a few minutes to fifteen minutes of practice a day to get a Cool Mind.

The term *Cool Mind* comes from an old saying: "with a cool mind and a warm heart." It means that when you act with a clear mind, care, and compassion, you'll make decisions that you and others will feel good about. A person with a Cool Mind is not at the mercy of his or her moods, not pushing hard against the flow of life, and not losing control with wild displays of emotion.

We are all born with a Cool Mind, but somewhere along the bumpy road of childhood we begin to cover it over with worries, fears, and concerns. We call this *conditioning,* and it's how we try to protect ourselves from scary emotions. The protective thought patterns stick, and as we move from childhood into adulthood, they just get in the way. In fact, most of the time they just stir up anxiety and other miserable stuff that keeps us stuck in our own drama.

Stress and anxiety mean that worry thoughts are going through your mind in a concentrated way; a Cool Mind will help you release these thoughts and allow you to let go of any worries. There are two main ways to reduce stress and worry in your life:

- Practice the habit of moving negative thinking to more logical, positive thoughts.

- Practice the art of relaxing your mind with meditation techniques.

Cultivating a consciously Cool Mind is, at least in theory, one of the simplest things you can do because you don't have to think. In fact, it's all about practicing the art of *not* thinking—or at least of not thinking negatively—if only for a few minutes at a time.

If you are wondering how it will ever be possible to "not think," consider the momentary calm when you sneeze. Sneezing stops thoughts in their tracks, which gives you a glimpse of a quiet mind. It's a calming moment. Coughing and yawning can have a similar effect. So does the presleep phase.

HOW CAN RELAXATION AND MEDITATION HELP ME?

Relaxation techniques are basically all about helping you to find your neutral feeling place. This is the place where there's just you and your body, without stress, without thinking. Your Cool Mind is a calm place, and you can find it any time you need to!

The art of relaxing and getting a Cool Mind lies

in learning how to let go. By letting go, you are dropping your resistance to the things that are causing you stress. The more you fight or dramatize the things in your life, the greater your stress. When you reduce your thoughts, you induce relaxation, and when you induce relaxation, you reduce your resistance. When you let go of negative thinking, you momentarily drop your resistance to life. That's what happens when you go to sleep—you let go and drop your resistance. And that's why sleep feels so good, particularly when you are stressed.

WON'T PEOPLE WALK ALL OVER ME IF I JUST LET GO?

Some people think that letting go, or dropping their resistance, must mean losing control. They think they'll become pushovers, but that's not true. Letting go *when you need to* is the key. Knowing when and how to release resistance to a stressor is what gives you control. A lack of stress does not mean a lack of caring—instead, it means having as clear a mind as possible to apply to the things you care about.

> Letting go doesn't mean losing control; it means gaining freedom!

Letting go is about realizing when to give up the thoughts and responses to life that are just causing you tension and worry, such as when you're faced with things you can't really change. For example, if it's an exam you're worried about, letting go of the stress and then returning to your studies with a clearer mind and a different outlook will empower you.

Cool Mind is about finding relief in any situation. Finding relief is the essential precondition of calm and happiness.

A Cool Mind will give you more control over your life, no matter what is going on around you. With a Cool Mind, you will perform more calmly and accurately, make better decisions, and look and feel healthier. People will act differently toward you because you will be more balanced and easy to be around.

REDUCING STRESS

Cultivating a Cool Mind reduces the stress that you experience from both outside sources and from within yourself. External stress can come from many places— school, exams, sports competitions, family issues, social situations, and so on. But here are a few ways we bring it on ourselves:

- Thoughts of being inadequate.
- Thoughts of being unworthy.
- Thoughts of being ugly.
- Thoughts of being stupid.
- Thoughts that the world will end if we don't get 95 percent on an exam.
- Thoughts that say, "They hate me."

Stressful feelings in your body are really alarm bells telling you that you have resistant thoughts to what is happening in your life. Stress can manifest itself in the body in many different ways, such as headaches, stomach and digestive problems, back pain, frequent colds, tiredness, difficulty thinking, and the inability to make decisions (the "don't know" mind). Stress urgently diverts the energy required to keep your mind and body healthy into fight-or-flight chemicals that, over the long term, run your system down.

When you think a thought, either good or bad, your body responds with a chemical to let your body "feel" the thought—it matches the thought to a bodily sensation. If the thought is "This is a disaster," your chest may tighten or you may feel sick. If the thought is a happy one, your body will feel light and loose. Think a panicky thought, and your body will create chemicals to make you feel panic. This is known as the fight-or-flight response because your body is making adrenaline to help you either stay and fight or flee. In the same way, calm and happy thoughts will make your body produce chemicals that enable you to feel calm and happy.

CONTROLLING ANGER AND ANXIETY

Studies have shown that angry thoughts create a physical feeling that produces even more anger. If anger is the appropriate emotion to help you express something or to make you act when something is just plain wrong—well, go for it. Just move through it quickly before you end up staying in an angry space and acting out your anger. But if anger is just the usual way you respond to stuff because you feel threatened when no threat really exists, then learning to take a deep breath and letting the anger go may turn your life around.

If you are often nervous or panicky, or you feel useless and full of doubt, your habitual thinking has brought you to that state in one way or another. If, in the middle of those feelings, you try to say positive things to yourself that you don't really believe, it won't help because you just won't believe them. What will help you, though, is to become aware of your unhelpful thoughts through meditation and other techniques. By doing this, you will soften your resistant thoughts and reduce their power so you can gain clarity.

In school and college, information goes into your head all day long. You have to draw on many thoughts as you learn in class, then you have to study and cram for exams. You are learning, expanding, learning, expanding all the time. It should be fun and interesting, but all too often it builds anxiety and pressure within you. For example, when you're a junior or senior in high school, you need certain grades to get into college. If the way you think about yourself is negative or your approach to exams is nerve-racking and makes you sick, then you're making it hard to perform well. You would benefit enormously by letting go of the thinking that trips you up. And the last thing you need to do is to stress about *how* to think when you're stressed.

A Cool Mind uses the opposite strategy: there's *nothing* to think about. You simply learn to slow down your thoughts, relax, and lessen your resistance. Just let life flow. How cool is that?

MEDITATION FOR A COOL MIND

Meditation is one major tool for developing a Cool Mind. There are countless descriptions of meditation, but the easiest way to think of it is "focusing the mind." Other similar terms would be contemplation, healing, and quieting the mind. Athletes and musicians enter a state of meditation when they perform, while a relaxed gardener tending to a rosebush could be said to be meditating. So if you have a relaxed mind and are singularly focused, then you're meditating.

Studies have shown that during meditation, the analytical part of your brain slows down, while the creative part actually speeds up. So if your head is always full of worries or unhelpful thoughts, some of the techniques in this book can help you find deep peace underneath all the mental chatter.

Trying to find a positive thought once worry has set in is often very hard to do and just requires more thinking. But meditation can help; taking a few seconds to cool yourself down when you face stress gives you a chance to stay calm and on top of whatever is happening. Meditation is not about reducing effort or taking things less seriously; it's about chilling out and then reinvesting your energy and efforts in a clearer, happier way.

What Will I Feel during Meditation?

It will be totally different for everyone, and the same person will have different experiences on any given day, but here are a few examples: tingling skin; itchiness; a deep feeling of peace; a softening of the muscles; an awareness of slow, deep breathing; moving or swaying. You may be more or less aware of any physical sensations you have. You could begin to feel incredibly powerful, vulnerable, or even slightly out of control. There might be a calm stillness in your mind that escapes as soon as you notice it. These are all normal feelings.

When you are gripped with stress and worry, you can . . .

- Let go of any physical and mental tension to improve your concentration and circulation.

- Let go of the thoughts that tell you your result is going to define you as a success or a loser.

- Let go and trust that your uncluttered mind will provide the intelligence and creativity you want, when you want it.

- Let go and know that whatever happens you are all-powerful.

- Let go and allow your body to heal and be healthy and free of tension.

How Can I Be Calm When There's So Much to Worry About?

Worrying about something gives it a chance to get bigger. It keeps both the worry itself and the habit of worrying alive.

Sometimes creating a drama keeps your "plight" visible and critical, but it does not offer any relief to the situation. If your worry habit is alive and well, you'll also find there will always be a new problem to replace any you solve! Believe it or not, once you begin to practice the techniques in this book, you'll find it is harder and takes more energy to stay stressed about something than it does to just let go of thinking.

When your thinking keeps causing you hassles over things that haven't even happened yet, you are "futuring" yourself negatively. Futuring yourself means that your mind has raced off to situations and hassles that haven't even happened yet—and may not ever happen (what a waste of energy!). It's basically

> **Putting relief in the space where stress was is the way to a Cool Mind.**

visualizing the future negatively and it scares you right out of the present moment. It's an easy habit to get into, but the good news is that it's also a habit we can break. It's time to learn to "defuture" yourself! "Defuture" means to simply be in the present moment, right here right now, just being your natural self. Having a cooler mind will help defuture you, or at least give you the chance to future yourself more positively. The more we know ourselves and our motivations, the more power and resolve we have to rise through the doubts and achieve whatever we want to accomplish.

THE BENEFITS OF GETTING CALM

Calm is the birthplace of happiness, the fountain of creativity, the key to your mental library, the cutting edge of invention, the access point to your intuition, the source of joy and good health, and the launching pad of inspired action. You *can* be at peace anytime you want, and when you are, you'll know what makes you tick, where you want to go, and what you want to do. Your actions will feel just right. Once you can find your Cool Mind, you will have the tools to keep going beyond your previous limits. You are who you are, and the sooner you are at peace with and excited by it, the sooner life will open up.

It often seems that it's the cool people we know who take all the risks and have all the adventures. We watch others confidently take chances, while our doubts and fears hold us back. The same thing can happen with learning and exams. When you walk into an exam, you take all the information that is rattling around inside your head and try to "bring it up" as you answer the questions. But if you are anxious or panicky, those thoughts hijack your ability to locate the right information. How often have you been in the shower or jogging later and—bang!—you're hit with the answer? You dropped your resistance without realizing it, and the answer presented itself.

How different would exam time feel if you could approach it with more calm and positive expectations?

One meditation teacher described the negative voice in our heads as a parrot perched on our shoulder, squawking all day long. "You can't do that, loser! Squawk! You're hopeless! Squawk!" So we will refer to that negative voice that sucks the fun out of life as our parrot. Your parrot will always resist a Cool Mind.

Once you begin to feel at home with the techniques in this book, you will also begin to have more choices and clarity about how you react to what's going on around you. From clarity and calm spring intuition, creativity, confidence, and happiness. From negative emotions spring anxiety, fear, anger, jealousy, and other feelings of doom. By practicing the techniques, you'll be able to cut down on the negative emotions, think about situations that used to be stressful in a more peaceful way, and nurture yourself. You'll be able to look at situations from a higher perspective—a more powerful place.

> Happiness and anxiety cannot exist at the same time.

Regardless of what is going on outside you, if you're happy on the inside, you're well ahead of the pack.

THE PATH TO HAPPINESS

Many people who don't have internal happiness need to go and get it somewhere else, usually in a manner that isn't good. You see it in bullies or vandals or kids who get hammered on booze—they are trying to find happiness outside themselves, while the reality is that they have endless happiness available on the inside.

Happiness increases your energy. Happy people radiate energy. You can see it in their eyes and posture. Negative states of mind, on the other hand, contract your body and pinch off your energy.

Being happy isn't complicated. If you've ever been seriously happy or content, you know that feeling when you smile like an idiot for no reason. The cool thing to know is that happiness is never far away or something that's always "out there." It is right here, right now—and you can find it. Real happiness, as the Dalai Lama says, "is built on the foundation of a calm, stable mind." Meditation puts you on that path.

HOW DO I GET A COOL MIND?

There's a saying that trees can't grow strong roots in a storm. You need to practice the art of relaxation when the weather is good so you can use it when the weather is bad!

Just as you have to play a sport repeatedly before you become proficient or learn algebra over time, the art of Cool Mind takes practice—specifically, meditation practice. The good news is that you only have to find a minimum of three minutes a day to begin. You can even clock them up accumulatively if you have to: say, one minute before you get up, one at lunchtime, and one before you go to bed. But you do need to do it every day and make it a habit to reap the full rewards. After you have been practicing for a while, you'll find it can take only seconds to reduce worry and bodily tension.

Three minutes a session (if it's committed time) is just enough to give you a taste of the unlimited benefits that meditation can bring. Three minutes of mental rest a day from your "parrot" can be a huge relief, especially if you are an anxious or nervous person. Fifteen minutes a day is nice if you can dedicate the time, but that might be difficult, so three minutes will get you into the game. It may be enough to introduce you to the "aha factor."

The aha factor is when you experience that little moment of realization or calm, or when you recognize that you're feeling good in a situation that would previously have stressed you out. Little moments like these are priceless.

In this book, I don't get into the scientific studies on how meditation works on your brain and body, because right now there is enough studying in your life as it is! But there are loads of positive research results out there on meditation if you want to look into them. Anyway, the best studying you can ever do on the benefits of meditation is to practice it and live the benefits. Make yourself the research project.

What You Can Gain from Meditation

Greater creativity

Better health

Better concentration

Increased decision-making ability

Improved memory

More energy

Enhanced physical and mental performance

More self-confidence

Better sleep

Higher levels of empathy

These concrete benefits of meditation will also help bring more peace, satisfaction, and positive relationships into your life.

What You Can Ditch with Meditation

Excess worry

Anxiety

Tight muscles

Complaining

Boredom

Confusion

Drama

Self-doubts

Negative self-talk

Self-obsession

As I've said, meditation is a practice, so there is a little bit of work to do on your part. You have to trust in yourself enough to let go, relax, and just breathe for at least a few minutes a day.

The next section of this book includes meditations to improve your concentration, help you tune in to your intuition, help you heal, give you power, help you just appreciate life more, and help you dream and feel inspired. Although they are all slightly different, these techniques all center around two main things: letting go and breathing! Some of them are an adaptation of meditations that have served countless people over thousands of years, helping them to quiet their minds and bringing them wisdom and happiness.

Whatever technique you ultimately decide to use, mindfulness—or being aware of the present moment—will be at the center of it. When you first begin practicing the techniques, you may not even notice that you have slipped into a daydream. So when that happens, don't beat yourself up, just come back to your chosen technique. Getting frustrated with yourself is one of the little speed bumps you have to get past on your way to Cool Mind. Getting frustrated with yourself is your bad old habit slipping in the back door to undermine you!

CHOOSING THE TECHNIQUE THAT'S BEST FOR YOU

Unless you are drawn to one technique in particular, do them in order and give each one a try for a few days to see how you feel. Some people feel immediate benefits from a particular style, while others take years to feel any benefit. Some meditators who have been practicing every day for twenty-five years still feel like beginners, so anything is possible for you.

Since right now we are mainly concerned with you feeling good, simply use the method that makes you feel the best. Always remember that it's not how well you do it that's important, but just that you are taking time out to do it. There is no doing well or not so well—it's just doing.

POSTURE

Sit in a position that helps your concentration and circulation. Slumped, lazy, or sleepy postures pinch off your energy and have no benefit. I often say, "Where your mind goes, your body goes," meaning that your thinking can affect how you're feeling. Good posture is a mark of dignity, and it's a good habit to bring your best posture to each session.

Sit comfortably with your spine upright and in its natural shape—it should look like an elongated *S*. In this position, your neck and shoulders can relax without strain, and your ribs can move freely, allowing you to breathe naturally. Any position that requires physical effort will only bring you tension, so keep it natural.

BREATHING

All meditation and relaxation programs work with your breath, so no matter what technique you choose, you should start by focusing on your breath. Why is this?

The main reason is that your breath is your most immediate connection to life: it is easy to locate in a hurry; you can feel it, hear it, draw it into certain parts of your body, and even see it in the winter. If you can't find your breath, staying "cool" is the least of your problems.

Your breathing rate also settles your heart rate, and if your heart rate is settled, *you* will be settled.

Deep breathing also keeps the oxygen circulating in your body clean so that it can dispel carbons that accumulate in your system.

> You shouldn't force the breath in any way; that only introduces tension.

Focused breathing settles your emotions, which in turn reduces the stress chemicals in your body, which settles your emotions further, and so on. So while you could say, "Breathing relaxes my body," you could also say, "An absence of breath makes me tense."

Concentrating on your breath gives you a quick snapshot of how tight your body is and how busy your head is. When you are stressed, your breathing rate may be an erratic one or two breaths a second, or you may just be holding it in. In deep calm, you may only take a breath every ten to twenty seconds.

How to Work the Breath

When you first start meditating, your breath—not your mind—is the leader, so all you need to focus on is letting your breath settle into whatever rhythm feels right. Give yourself the time and permission to relax into the rhythm of breathing. Just watch it; be a spectator.

Just feel your body rise and fall with your breath. Imagine that you have just hopped onto the couch to relax and watch TV; you settle in, get comfortable, and see what comes on. Here, you settle down, take a breath, and see what your body and mind are doing right now. Don't go into any thoughts or feelings you may have. Just observe and relax into your breathing rate as it is.

Try placing your tongue against the roof of your mouth to relax your neck, and if your attention wanders, the next thing you'll realize is that your tongue is on the floor of your mouth. When did that happen?

Breathe in and out through your nose, and when you feel settled, you're ready to begin your technique.

THE TECHNIQUES

1

COOL MINDFULNESS

Best for:

> Improving concentration
>
> Developing mental focus
>
> Calming your mind
>
> Quieting your thoughts
>
> Following your breath

You may have heard *mindfulness* described as "living in the moment." But what does that mean exactly?

Living in the moment means to be fully aware of right now. Your body may be here, but where are your thoughts? Most of the time we have thoughts rattling around in our heads about our plans for Saturday night or an exam we're going to flunk—basically, the same sort of thinking that got us stressed in the first place.

As I pointed out earlier, a lot of our stress comes from "future thinking," or worrying about things that haven't happened yet—particularly when we future think negatively and see ourselves crashing and burning in advance. (If you happen to future think positively, then don't change a thing!)

We need to think ahead, sure, but a lot of our future thinking causes us to become anxious. Mindfulness helps us be more aware of what we're thinking *right now.*

If you are in the habit of futuring yourself negatively, then you are rehearsing for things to go badly. But if you currently think about things negatively and then they turn out negatively, isn't it possible that if you got in the habit of seeing things positively, then your outcomes could be positive?

Sometimes, rather than finding the right thought to think, it's easier to just go to the breath and notice that the negative thoughts are active. Realizing they are there is the best way to neutralize them, because you can either let them go or try a slightly improved thought.

Try this: close your eyes and think about all the blue things in the room. Then think about all the red things. What were they? This is being mindful. If you came into the room feeling stressed, I bet you didn't notice anything. When you are stressing about something, you often don't notice the good stuff all around you.

Mindfulness creates a tiny gap between what happens in life and your response to it. In this little gap is the potential for self-improvement.

Here's how to find it.

Sit cross-legged on the floor, or sit tall in a chair.

If you're on the floor, shove a cushion underneath your bottom to reduce the tension in your legs.

Let your hands lie relaxed in your lap, or make them into loose fists and rest them on top of your knees.

Keep your eyes open and gaze at the ground about two feet in front of you—your gaze should be soft, as if you are looking through the floor. If the eye-open method is difficult, then close your eyes, but stay as alert to your breath as you can. If you go to sleep easily, it may be best to keep your eyes open for a few minutes.

Before you start, give yourself permission to relax your mind and body. You can use phrases on your out-breath like, "letting go," "I'm letting go easily," "releasing thoughts, relaxing the body," or you can try the shorter

Tip: Say the words to yourself silently or very quietly. There is no need to voice them out loud.

version which is, "release on the in-breath, relax on the out-breath." This method really works for a busy mind because it keeps you focused on the rhythm of the words. As you breathe in, you say "release"; as you breathe out, you say "relax." These phrases bring attention and respect to the meditation and yourself.

As thoughts arise, just notice them, let them go, and come back to your breath. The thoughts may seem important but know that you can come back to them later. For the next few minutes, you have given yourself permission to relax mentally.

With this style of mindfulness meditation, you just concentrate on the feeling of the breath, the depth of it, the clearing of your lungs, and the softening of your body. Become curious as to how breathing feels, since each breath is unique.

If you are having trouble with a wandering mind, you can try counting your breaths, which will give you a focus. Breathe slowly in through your nose, then count silently as you exhale: one . . . two . . . three . . .

four, then start over. You count to four and return to one so you don't get lost in a game to see how high you can count—that's just another way to be busy.

Another option is to say "two" as you breathe in, since that can soften that empty space between the in-breath (inhalation) and the out-breath (exhalation).

For some people, counting the breath can introduce tension into their session. If that is how you're feeling, forget it, let it go, and try another style!

You can either just breathe for as long as you feel comfortable—anywhere from a few minutes up to fifteen—or you can do three to five sets of four breaths with a little break in between each set, and build up your practice that way.

Once you are relaxed and your breathing is settled, you can also experiment with combining an out-breath of seven seconds with an in-breath of five seconds. That way you can simply think of nothing except the breath counts.

Don't force yourself to concentrate, since this only causes anxiety. Just relax, enjoy the fact that your mind is cooling off, and keep returning to your breath.

2

COOL RELAXATION

Best for:

> Calming your mind
>
> Releasing tension in your body
>
> Practicing breathing
>
> Letting go
>
> Recovering from exercise

If your mind is too full and busy to slow down, work on relaxing your body, and your mind will tag along.

Remember, where the mind goes, the body goes. This is also a great technique to help release physical stress from the body. Plus, since you'll be lying down, you'll have gravity on your side to help you out.

Here's how to do it: Lie on the ground with your knees up and your feet flat on the floor (or lie completely flat if you can do this and stay alert). Place your hands on the sides of your rib cage, in line with your bottom ribs, and encourage your breath to wander down to where your hands are. You should feel your ribs moving slightly outward rather than up and down.

As you breathe, scan your body; wherever you find tension, just imagine letting it go. Allow the tension to melt away. If it won't, let it be, relax the rest of your body, and check in with the stubborn spot later.

Say to yourself, "I can relax easily. It comes naturally." Go with it. Let your nerves and muscles unwind, and sink into the floor. Let gravity do its thing. Let your mind just observe your body relaxing. Your spine will grow heavier as your nerves relax and the tension drains away like melting ice.

Instead of scanning your body and relaxing tension where you find it, you can begin at your feet and move slowly up your body, if you prefer. Focus on your feet, mentally scanning each one and imagining the tension melting away. Move up through your calf muscles and thighs. Make your way to your belly, and imagine your stomach walls giving way to calm. Move up through your heart to your neck and isolate the muscles around your mouth, jaw, eyes, and forehead. This can take anywhere from three to twenty minutes, depending on your focus and available time. It often helps to flex the muscle you are focusing on and then sink into the feeling of it relaxing again.

Here's another version you can try: With your eyes open, imagine peering through a spot on the ceiling. (This means you gaze at the spot softly like you are looking at something just behind it.) If you must close your eyes, keep the concentration on the breath until you get comfortable, then work through the tension-releasing steps we have just covered.

The phrase "letting go" is a good thing to repeat a few times as you begin, but avoid telling yourself to "let go," since that can sound like you're giving an order. If you're having trouble relaxing, mentally barking, "*Let go!*" will probably end the session right there.

Your body wants to feel energy pumping through it, but it needs to relax and recover. Your muscles and nerves need to soften so the tension in your body can dissolve before it builds up. Be aware, though, that it's easy to drop off to sleep or slip into a daydream if you stay in this meditation for too long, so watch out for that!

3

COOL VISUALIZATIONS

Best for:

      Relaxing

      Developing creativity

      Stimulating your imagination

      Empowering yourself

      Energizing your body

The power you can generate from deep visualization is unlimited. Fortunately, visualizing comes easily to most of us who like to spend time daydreaming. And if you can daydream, you can visualize.

You can create anything you want during visualization, so it's a wonderful imagination tool, and it's most effective when you visualize as vividly as possible. Enliven it with all the sights, sounds, feelings, and sensations that you can imagine until it comes to life within you.

Visualizing is a great tool for anything ranging from relaxing to empowering yourself, from healing to preparing yourself for a tough situation. You can do it lying down in a comfortable position or just as easily sitting at a desk. Soft music can help to create a good mood for visualization.

When you're ready, just close your eyes, give yourself permission to let go, and see yourself in the perfect environment you want to create. Go as deep into your place of calm as you can and feel every bit of it—the temperature, the water, the rain, the sun, the mountain mist—and hear every sound—the birds, the waterfalls, the waves.

The aim of this style of meditation is to bring those feelings of calm or power to what you are doing now. Walk away from each of these sessions with the memory of how you felt during your visualization.

Here are some examples that will help you make up your own.

EXAMPLE 1

You are walking through a rainforest. The sun is splintering through the treetops, and the birds are chirping away. You come across a stream and sit on the bank. The morning sun is bright but not too hot, and the dew has just about gone from the grass. As you sit, a fish jumps and splashes near you, and the resulting ripple widens across the water. You look closely at the water; what other fish are in there?

EXAMPLE 2

You are the Almighty, the Creator. You sit on top of your mountain or under your waterfall or float down your river and breathe in the power of it. You are in vibrant good health, and you have perfect, positive energy. You rejuvenate in your kingdom.

EXAMPLE 3

Let a time come to mind when someone poured plenty of love or care into you. Go right into it and immerse yourself in the feelings that come up. If nothing comes up or you don't have those memories, make it up or imagine you are doing it for a baby. Imagine how that baby feels. Finish by dropping the thoughts and staying with the physical feelings.

EXAMPLE 4

You dive into a stream, and the current wants to carry you with it. You feel safe, so it's no big deal. You start to relax and let it take you. The more you go with it, the more you relax, and you realize that the stream is only taking you deeper into paradise. You completely let go and trust the stream completely. You can bring the lesson of not struggling so much back to reality with you.

EXAMPLE 5

You are on a beach at sunrise, and nobody is around. You are doing a few stretches or some yoga, listening to the waves and watching as they sparkle in the sunlight. You start off on a walk, then build up speed until it turns into a jog on the sand. You have never felt so light and strong. You are running effortlessly across the sand. Take in the power.

4

COOL PERFORMANCES

Best for:

> Enhancing any type of performance
>
> Improving concentration
>
> Developing mental focus
>
> Facilitating rehearsals
>
> Building confidence

A lot of research shows that the subconscious mind does not know the difference between what is vividly imagined and what is real. If you can imagine it, you can create it. Nervous and panicky thoughts stifle you and don't allow you to show off your natural talents. You end up getting in your own way. So it's advantageous to mentally rehearse every bit of a performance you have coming up.

Whether it's a musical piece, a speech, a gymnastics performance, or a rowing competition, mentally go through the entire performance in vivid detail, imagining exactly how you want it to unfold. You will benefit by running through this visualization as often as you can, well before the performance—even weeks before. By the time you hit the stage, you want to feel like you've done it a thousand times already. You only have to be cool and let your talent do the rest.

Here's how to do it: Get yourself into a comfortable position, either sitting up or lying down, and then breathe yourself into relaxation.

When your mind and body are calm, begin the perfect performance visualization from the very beginning. Imagine yourself getting ready that morning, confident and excited. Get your bags together. Get to the track or theater. Feel the perfectly normal tingling in your spine and the flow of energy in your veins. Go to the starting line or stage full of concentration and determination. Go through the entire race or act in real time just as you want it to happen.

Another great way to overcome any nerves or doubts is to fully understand why you are

Make your performance feel good and always finish while it's feeling good. Don't hang around in the visualization longer than that. If any situation other than a good one appears, don't try too hard to correct it. Just start fresh.

doing the thing you want to do. If you are feeling nervous about something but know why you are going to do it, you can find great strength in focusing on these reasons.

Relax for a couple of minutes with some breathing exercises, then ask yourself why you do this activity. View the question as an interested spectator and see what comes up. There may be nothing magical in the answer you get other than that you're trying to have fun, but to know your answer can be very calming. If you come to understand why you play music, debate, run, and so on, you'll always be able to find motivation and a reason to overcome any doubts.

5

COOL POWER

Best for:

>Empowering yourself
>
>Energizing your body
>
>Preparing for sports
>
>Getting physically well
>
>Building confidence

This is a great technique from the Reiki tradition to get you feeling more powerful and energized. Reiki is a Japanese word—*rei* means "spiritual," and *ki* means "energy." It is used to enhance the speed of your internal energy to increase your sense of well-being and your energy level.

Begin by sitting comfortably, let your thoughts go, and relax into the breath.

Lie down and place your hands across your stomach near your navel. Imagine breathing in a color, say red, and draw the color down to your navel where your hands are resting. Imagine the color giving you much-needed energy and strength. With your mind, follow the feelings of energy spreading and filling your body—in through your nose, down through your neck, and around your navel. Breathe in energy, and breathe out tension. Follow the breath in this way until you feel energized but calm.

Use whatever color comes most easily to mind, but as a general guide, reds and oranges are the most energetic colors, and white is the purest and most versatile. (See page 102 for more information on how to use colors.)

6

COOL HEALING

Best for:

        Healing

        Nurturing

        Rejuvenating

        Relaxing

To be healthy and stay healthy, the energy in your body needs to circulate. So when you want to heal something in yourself, you need to relax and let your body do its thing with the natural energy you produce.

When you're not feeling your best, there are many ways to stimulate your body's natural healing process.

Start by either sitting in a meditation pose or lying flat. Allow your body to relax and your mind to let go. Place one hand on your belly and the other on your chest so you feel centered and supported. This also "connects" you to two of the main energy centers of your body: the belly and the heart. As you relax, get a sense of the warmth and energy building up around your hands and torso. You can also visualize breathing in an outside "energy" of some sort to further enhance your own healing energy. This could be the color red from the earth's center, a powerful energy from the Universe, or something you make up on your own. You can send this energy to the part of your body that needs healing either by focusing your mental attention on it or by putting your hands on the area.

As you begin to relax, you can also silently repeat phrases like "My body is healing perfectly," or "My body knows how to heal perfectly."

If you want to use a visualization to help yourself heal, it is best to visualize the injured or sick part of your body as perfectly healthy.

Remember: circulation is the key to healing, and the key to circulation is being unrestricted in your mind and body. So relax and trust that your body knows what to do!

7

COOL WALKING

Best for:

> Clearing your mind quickly
>
> Unwinding
>
> De-stressing
>
> Increasing enjoyment of everyday activities
>
> Feeling appreciative

No time to meditate? Try this. Walking meditation puts your mind in a cool place pretty quickly, and sometimes you know that walking from one place to another is all the time you're going to get to yourself.

This walking meditation comes from the Vietnamese Zen monk, Thich Nhat Hanh. When you are walking—rather than hurrying—somewhere, deepen your breath and take seven mindful steps in appreciation or gratitude for something in your life. Walking mindfully means that your focus is simply on the act of walking. You walk, aware of your breathing and life around you. Someone on a smartphone who walks into a parked car is not walking mindfully!

Here are some other walking meditations:

Take seven steps with full mindfulness and feeling for your ancestors, grandparents, or someone who has recently died so they still feel like part of you. Bring the best memories that you have of them into your thoughts. It's easy to dedicate seven mindful steps to someone or something meaningful.

Take seven steps for the air you breathe, your body, the trees, or someone who is ill. Take seven steps for all the things you're grateful for and another seven for yourself because you're doing pretty well in life.

Breathe with total mindfulness of how each footstep feels. Seriously, how does it feel? How far up your leg does the pressure of each step go? Do you feel the pressure through each foot evenly?

If you are walking between exams or to meet a date, you have done all you can do—there's no time to study further or make yourself look more attractive. So just surrender and be mindful of staying calm and keeping your mind clear. Find your cool place in your footsteps by focusing on the technique of mindful walking as described in this exercise. The more you can focus on your technique, the less your analytical mind will trip you up.

8

COOL CLARITY

Often when we're under pressure, we just plain lose it! At that point, we're back in our old reptile brain, which is all about "fight mode." It makes us feel like we're five years old again, and that's not helpful, particularly in situations when we need to keep thinking clearly. If we need to stay creative, logical, cool, and calm, we need both the left and right sides of our brain to work in harmony.

The left side of the brain is the logical, analytical side and works in words, while the right side is mostly creative and intuitive and works in pictures. When we *lose control* or have strong emotions, we lose the balance between the two hemispheres and over-activate one side more than the other. When this happens, solving problems and seeing things clearly becomes very difficult.

So if you need a clear mind in any situation— before an exam, before you do homework, or before participating in sports—you can try doing this exercise for a couple of minutes or until you feel more relaxed and focused.

The beauty of the whole-brain technique is that you can do it while walking, sitting, standing, or lying down. Because the left brain controls the right side of the body and the right brain controls the left side of the body, it's simply a matter of crossing your right hand and foot over your left hand and foot. Cross your wrists over each other, then interlock your fingers with your palms pressed together, but not too tightly because you don't want to be creating any more tension. Cross your ankles too—unless you are walking, of course. If you are sitting or lying down, just close your eyes and let your breathing deepen until your emotions settle. Don't force your breathing, though; it will happen naturally. If you are walking, it will still be a big help to cross your wrists and lock your fingers. If this is a sports situation, simply tap your right hand anywhere on the left side of your body and your left hand anywhere on the right side of your body.

9

COOL FOCUS

Best for:

      De-stressing quickly

      Relaxing

      Improving concentration

Noise can actually be a good thing to meditate on, so don't treat it as an irritation if it turns up halfway through your session. Instead, use noise as a tool to help you improve your ability to focus. Noise from fans and refrigerators in particular are very consistent, so they are easy to meditate to—turn them into a positive. If you're lucky, you'll get to meditate on the sound of rain, since that is one of the best noises of all.

Another way to use noise to help in your practice of mindfulness is to sit with your eyes closed and try to follow a sound until it fades completely. Follow the noise of a passing train until it fades away. Listen to a bird's song until it flies off.

Alternatively, sit and concentrate on how many types of noises you can hear. If you're feeling nervous or are waiting for something to begin, it can be calming to close your eyes, take a few breaths, and focus on the sounds around you. How many different people's voices do you hear? How many bird calls can you pick up?

After a while, you should be comfortable relaxing to the sound of barking dogs!

This technique can also be used with sight. Instead of closing your eyes and focusing on a sound, watch a bird fly until it disappears or watch a surfer catch a wave and ride it right in to shore.

You can also use sight to focus on feeling. Take an object—a tennis ball, a sweater, or a piece of fruit—and place it on the floor just in front of you. Gaze softly at the object and begin to feel it, just as if you were holding it. In your mind, turn it around, squeeze it, catch it, feel the weight and texture of it. Stay focused on the object for as long as you can. You can also consider the life of the object. How many hands has it been through? Who made it? Who transported it? What were their stories?

If you don't have an object, think of one and stay with it for three to five minutes. Keep a tennis ball firmly in mind and watch it wherever it goes in your thoughts.

10

COOL GRATITUDE

Best for:

> Feeling happier about a situation
>
> Feeling appreciative
>
> Feeling loved
>
> Developing compassion

Make yourself comfortable and begin to focus on the breath. Once you have relaxed, turn your attention to things you can appreciate or for which you are grateful.

For example, you might feel appreciation for a teacher or relative who has helped you out recently, for a gift you have received, or for something as simple and abundant as the sunshine. It might sound corny, but meditations on these sorts of positive things can give you an enormous lift.

Appreciation is just a great way to start and finish the day. It feels good, and it will give you a boost in the morning. Being around appreciative people is energizing, so don't be surprised if other people are drawn to you. If you do this meditation before bed, there's a good chance you'll kick off the next morning in this frame of mind as well.

11

COOL RELEASE

Best for:

>Relaxing
>
>Relieving anxiety and stress
>
>Loosening up
>
>Clearing your head
>
>Energizing your body

This is a quick-release technique for dumping bodily tension wherever you are. It comes from the ancient Chinese health art of qi gong.

If you're just hanging out while waiting to begin a performance or competition, or if you're waiting outside the interview or exam room or your date's front door, do this technique to quickly reduce physical tension, help you chill a little, and let you think more clearly.

Close your eyes or leave them open, whichever you prefer, and imagine a wave of energy. This energy can be in the form of a color, a light, or a cloud. Have it start at your head and move it slowly down your body—how slowly depends on how much time you have, but the slower the better. As it passes through, it melts the tension around your head, into your neck, and down to your feet.

The wave then comes back up to your head and passes down again. Each time, the tension should travel down from your head and body and through your feet, as if it's going to liquefy on the floor. Imagine at the end of your session that there is a puddle of stress and tension left on the floor when you walk away.

Always make sure that the tension goes down through your feet and not up through your head. You don't want to make the mistake of pushing tension into your head until your brain hurts! You also don't want to be interrupted halfway through and be left with a head full of stress. Melting or dissolving downward is the way to get rid of the tension.

Practice this anywhere, anytime. You can even do it several times during the day as a way of observing how tense you are.

EXTRA STUFF

IN CASE OF AN EMERGENCY

In all cases of sudden stress, the breath is always the first place to go while you settle down a little. Here are a few other suggestions for handling stressful situations.

Example 1

If you're in a situation where it feels like the sky is falling or you're under threat, first put some space between you and the fear, close your eyes, and take a few deep breaths. Let the breath flow in and out at exactly the speed it wants to. Let it slow down at its own rate.

If you have a second to do so, check in with yourself. "Hi, nerves. I've got you, it's cool," or similar words, can help you get some calm back.

Naming the feelings—"I'm feeling nervous," or "There is fear going on here"—can help you settle down. Stick with words that describe your feelings rather than branding *yourself* with another label.

Go to your preferred technique (this is where it pays to have practiced), knowing you have a Cool Mind place to go to. You can also put your hand on your forehead and with your thumb and middle finger press above each eyebrow—these are the emotional stress release (ESR) points, and applying pressure to these points is a way of relieving tension. (You may have noticed that people often put their palms on their forehead when under stress.)

Example 2

The speech or performance you were dreading has come. You're walking up to the stage, there is no escape, and all you want to do is run.

The golden rule in a stressful situation is to meet the feelings with your breath. Always go to the breath in any challenging situation. Trust that things will turn out as they turn out and that you're more than capable of handling that.

It is in these challenging situations that you get the chance to really grow. These are the best times to practice being in control, to trust your natural talent. The more you do that, the stronger your belief in yourself will become. It will take many attempts before you begin to feel more comfortable, so be cool with yourself if the first few tries don't work out too well. If your self-belief doesn't come up to the mark, that's okay. Your Cool Mind is happy regardless.

The breath is the gateway to Cool Mind. A few

breaths will keep the stress chemicals from reproducing in your body and will enable you to trust yourself. Basically, focusing on your breathing will help you get out of your own way. Have you ever surprised yourself by doing something awesome and saying, "Wow, I didn't know I could do that!" That's because you got out of the way and happily focused on the task at hand. The possibilities are endless if we follow our gut feelings and get out of our own way.

Example 3

Things have gone horribly wrong; you're shaking and feeling like you could puke.

When a situation hits you forcefully, do whatever you can to feel better right now. Breathe, use the ESR points on your forehead (see example 1), leave, take a quick walk, move around—do whatever brings you some relief.

There's nothing to figure out at this point, as your head has probably caved in already. However, know that the "mind" that reacted strongly isn't the same "mind" that will decide what to do next. In the meantime, just try to feel better physically as soon as possible.

It's good to know that, if you've been practicing meditation, there is a place of calm within you when you need it. If these situations happen often, the fear of freaking out can become greater than the fear of the situation itself. So knowing that you can restore your Cool Mind through meditation is your ticket to taking on those fears little by little.

Talk to someone or get help as soon as you can, because letting high-stress events swirl around in your head just builds the pressure.

Example 4

You're just standing around when suddenly, "Oh no, here he/she is, walking over to me! I should ask him/her out." And then the "head talk" starts—usually badly.

"I can't ask her out, I'm an idiot."

"I'm totally uncool and ugly too."

"She'll laugh at me."

If your head talk is negative like this, just keep saying, "So what?" to yourself. There's no need to say anything more complex.

"I can't ask her out, I'm an idiot."

"So what?"

"I'm totally uncool and ugly too."

"So what?"

"She'll laugh at me."

"So what?"

She or he is probably more nervous than you are anyway, but you don't need to tell yourself that. "So what?" will do.

Keep saying it until you let go and do the thing you want to do with a "So what?" attitude. This works for just about any challenge you might find yourself facing. It puts the fears back in their place with a bit of comic relief. We often take ourselves too seriously, so this helps to clear the way.

Example 5

Imagine a situation that you are really not looking forward to. Visualize it in all its ugliness. Play it out in your mind and see how the situation feels to you. Not that great?

Now play it out positively and see how it feels. Better? That's how your life wants it to play out. Take that natural feeling into the situation and watch what happens.

If you are heading home one day, and you know there is a hassle waiting for you that you have to deal with, practice the positive visualization beforehand. Then take that feeling and mood into the situation and be patient with the outcome. If you present yourself to the situation with a positive attitude, you will create an atmosphere where things may have a better chance of working out for you.

HURDLES

Your Parrot

"I can't do it. I'm just no good at it." That's your parrot getting to you before you give yourself a chance. If this happens, just give yourself credit for taking a few minutes out and for noticing that your mind is racing and unsettled. It's normal. Be gentle, relax with the feeling that your mind is racing, and just watch. That's the best way to start.

Your parrot has probably been happily running the show for some years now and has enjoyed getting you into all sorts of bad mental states, so don't expect it to take kindly to being shut down. It will have all the excuses: "I'm too tired"; "It's dumb"; "I don't need this"; "I've got better things to do"; and so on. Be aware of your parrot complaining and just allow it to squawk in the background.

The Naysayers

In the early stages of practice, don't talk too much about your meditation unless you really want to share it with people close to you. If you tell too many people, you can be sure there will be someone who wants to shoot you back down to where you were. And if you're gaining benefits from your practice, the last thing you'll want is someone squashing your cloud.

The Worrying Mind

This is when you always think you have to figure something out. You sit down to relax, then in comes your mind, obsessing about something. It can be useful to realize that this type of thinking creates the stress in the first place. It is great practice to recognize unhelpful thinking and know that by putting it on hold while you relax, you can help break the habit.

Your Phone

It's a good idea to lose the phone or turn it off and put it where you can't see it—even when you're expecting a call. People will leave a message or call back.

No Time to Meditate

Sorry, that's your parrot talking. Remember, there is a technique to fit any situation, no matter how tight your time constraints are.

Procrastination

You have some heavy problems to sort out, and you'll start meditating when that's done. No way! The best time to practice is when you feel you're in the thick of things. It's when you can practice feeling calm *during* times of stress that you know you've made a leap forward. When you see through that excuse, you're well on your way to calm.

Unrealistic Expectations

Be patient and realistic. Don't expect rainbows or angels to appear after a few attempts. Cool Mind will flow slowly into your life as your practice deepens, and it will surprise you when it does.

No Quiet Place

Remember, there is a technique for anywhere and anytime. Begin with a couple of techniques and do them while walking, in the shower, or whenever you can grab a few seconds on your own.

I've Had Some Real Growth and I Don't Get Worried Anymore!

There is always a new challenge in life, and there will always be room for personal growth. Keep in mind that as you grow and change as a person, you may need to adapt the techniques you use or find new techniques. There is always a place for meditation and Calm Mind in your life.

COOL ACCESSORIES

Working with Colors

This may sound bizarre, but colors have electromagnetic qualities that we respond to unknowingly. Think about how the colors of things affect you: the color of your bedroom, your sports team's colors, your clothing colors. Do people say you look good in red but black doesn't suit you?

Here is a quick look at some colors and how they may affect you if you wear them or are surrounded by them.

Blue

Blue is a calming color for the emotions and is known to be inspiring and spiritual. It is also endless and vast—think blue sky or the ocean. If you are often fired up or have trouble relaxing, you might need some blue around you.

Green

The color of nature and growth, green is good for healing and calming the nerves. Think rain forests, green grass, and gardens.

Black

This is a deep color that has an air of mystery. It's thoughtful and creative but not big on fun and calm.

Yellow

Yellow is light-hearted, easy to look at, and full of happy, expressive energy. It is good for energizing and expressing yourself. Think morning sun and banana energy.

Orange

Orange is great for energizing and powering up. It will make your appetite kick in and is good for creativity. Think fresh oranges and long afternoons full of sun.

Brown

Brown is a solid color that reflects the earth. Stable and serious people get into brown. It's not great for your sense of humor, but it will get your feet on the ground if you live in dreamland. Think soil.

Gray

Gray is a mature color, which is neutral and good for thinking. It is not overly energizing, but it's good for time alone. Think calming rain clouds.

White

White is pure, clean, and heavenly. It is great for mental clarity. Think puffy clouds.

Red

Red is the most energetic and fiery of colors. It won't help you sleep well, but it will help you shake off your blues. Think fire and racy convertibles.

A FINAL WORD

The calm is always there, always within you, but you can't read about it to know it. Nobody can tell you about it, it's like the taste of an apple—you don't get to savor it by reading about it. You have to experience the calm within you in order to know it!

So, now over to you . . .

David Keefe is a mindfulness counselor and fitness coach from Sydney, Australia, and co-owner of Trinity Health and Fitness with his wife, Jane. He runs Cool Mind workshops for middle school and high school students in the Australian school system. He is also a practitioner of Zen and qi gong.